Mateus Barreiro

Freud and Schopenhauer: the unconscious and the notion of the non-conscious

Mateus Barreiro

Freud and Schopenhauer: the unconscious and the notion of the non-conscious

Epistemology of psychoanalysis

ScienciaScripts

Imprint

Cover image: www.ingimage.com

This book is a translation from the original published under ISBN 978-620-2-03440-1.

Publisher:
Sciencia Scripts
is a trademark of
Dodo Books Indian Ocean Ltd. and OmniScriptum S.R.L publishing group

120 High Road, East Finchley, London, N2 9ED, United Kingdom
Str. Armeneasca 28/1, office 1, Chisinau MD-2012, Republic of Moldova, Europe
Managing Directors: Ieva Konstantinova, Victoria Ursu
info@omniscriptum.com

Printed at: see last page
ISBN: 978-620-8-37683-3

Freud and Schopenhauer: the unconscious and the notion of the non-conscious

Mateus de Freitas Barreiro

Psychologist at PUC-Campinas, with a Scientific Initiation scholarship from the São Paulo State Research Foundation (FAPESP). He is studying for a PhD in Education at UNESP-Marilia. He is currently a lecturer in the Department of Psychology and Psychoanalysis at the State University of Londrina (UEL). He works in the areas of Epistemology of Psychoanalysis, Philosophy of Psychoanalysis and Philosophy of Education.

Summary

1 PREFACE

When discussing the relationship between Freud and Schopenhauer, there are various polemics about the extent to which Schopenhauer was an intellectual forerunner when he addressed the irrational aspects that do not make up the field of consciousness, creating fertile ground for the birth of psychoanalysis. The aim here is to support the idea that Schopenhauer's empirical experiences place him as an important protagonist when discussing the question of the unconscious. In his works, there are several indications of his practical work with patients at the Charite hospital in Berlin. For Schopenhauer, madness is a mechanism for forgetting traumatic experiences, but it should be emphasized that the relationship with the Freudian concept of repression goes far beyond Schopenhauer's empirical experience. The aim of this work is therefore to carry out a cross-sectional study, juxtaposing Freud's cardinal concepts with Schopenhauer's ideas, especially with regard to the encounters and disagreements that the prefix meta has in Schopenhauer's metaphysics and Freud's metapsychology.

2 INTRODUCTION

At the end of the nineteenth century, new paradigms flowed across the German cultural horizon with Schopenhauer and Nietzsche, as reason no longer occupied a sovereign place in man's mental faculties. Previously, in the history of philosophy, there was no shortage of allusions to non-conscious mental processes, and the unknowable was discussed by various philosophers. However, this was not the central axis of his postulates.

Freud's connection with Schopenhauerian thought is established through multiple points and forms of contact. Firstly, when Freud was developing his psychoanalytic theory, Schopenhauer's thought was pervasive at the end of the 19th century, and it was also very popular in the circles Freud frequented. Zentner reinforces Rank's point by evoking biographical data retrieved by Willian McGrath, in which he describes Freud's inclusion in a group of students called the German Students' Reading Club in Vienna between 1873-1878; one of the main authors studied in this group was Schopenhauer (ZENTNER, 1995). Schopenhauer's philosophy took many identifiable and unidentifiable paths into Freud's thoughts, thoughts that were also already filled with other types of ideas and knowledge from his psychoanalytic practice. All these intersections of knowledge, [including Schopenhauerian metaphysics, allowed both Freud and Schopenhauer to be part of the atmosphere in which psychoanalytic theory was created. In Lecture 35 of the *New Lectures,* Freud comments on the difference between philosophy and psychoanalysis, saying that the former consists of "an intellectual construction which resolves in a unitary way all the problems of our existence on the basis of a subsumed hypothesis, in which, consequently, no question remains open, and everything that retains our interest finds its determined place" (FULGENCIO, 2001 apud FREUD, 1933/1955d)[1] . But what does Freud himself think about the intersection of philosophy and psychoanalysis? For Freud, is it possible to combine philosophy with psychoanalysis?

Freud's contrast with philosophy involves the idea of a system of knowledge, a branch of knowledge, a discipline, psychoanalysis. The approach to philosophy should always be made with the reference that philosophy and psychoanalysis set out to achieve different goals, even if they are intertwined by some concepts that aim to answer other questions. When it comes to this interlocution of knowledge, covering Freud's relationship with philosophy, most of the time the theme refers to Freud's[2] ambivalence in relation to philosophy, since Freud sometimes neglects philosophy and in other circumstances reveres it for his old desire to be a philosopher.[3]

---

[1] Freud isn't referring to one philosopher in particular when it comes to philosophy's single-minded approach to solving problems.

[2] For Freud, delirium and philosophical discourse work in a similar way, because in both, subjectivity articulates words as if they were things, and there is no concern with subjecting discourse to the imperative of reality testing (BIRMAN, 2003).

[3] "In short, Freud stated that he was finally realizing his desire to be a philosopher with the

But what can we say about this ambivalent relationship with philosophy in Freud?

These questions were probably not intended to solve problems that permeated psychoanalytic practice, or even to resolve a relevant philosophical issue. Fulgencio (2003) makes a constructive comment on Freud's ambiguity in relation to philosophy. He suggests that this ambiguity does not refer to Freud's eminently practical work, as he always placed himself in the position of a scientist, seeking to solve empirical problems that required speculation, but his ultimate goal was to solve these problems and not to formulate a "world view" or crystallized truths about the world and man (FULGENCIO, 2003). Freud's aim, then, was not to answer philosophical questions, but to use philosophy to help create his psychoanalytic concepts.

Schopenhauer's concept of madness was one of the foundations that enabled Freud to create the concept of repression, to explain it in its development, with its respective topical, economic and dynamic points of view. Through the concept of madness, Freud was able to abstract beyond what his clinical practice brought him.

In the light of the above, the aim of this book is to warn against the risks of drawing an analogy between philosophy and psychoanalysis, with the aim of sustaining a possible

---

invention of psychoanalysis" (BIRMAN, 2003).

reductionism of psychoanalysis in relation to philosophy or ignoring any influences of philosophy in relation to psychoanalysis. However, the aim of this work is to understand the existence of continuity between the thoughts of Schopenhauer and Freud, although each of them has its own characteristics, which culminated in the development of different specific criteria for validating knowledge in their respective fields of knowledge, Given that Schopenhauer was the philosopher most often cited by Freud, the meetings and disagreements concerning the methodological foundations that underpinned the theses of each author will be explored in depth, especially how the notion of the non-conscious and unconscious was approached by Freud and Schopenhauer. The assumption that philosophy has disregarded thoughts that escape consciousness is not something seen in the history of philosophy. The notion of the non-conscious needs to be analyzed according to its time and the conditions that permeate Freud's and Schopenhauer's life history. Thinking about how a thought unfolds in different fields of knowledge and different epochs, we will briefly illustrate how the notion of the non-conscious was worked on in other epochs and contexts prior to psychoanalysis.

3 EMOTIONS AND THE NOTION OF THE NON-CONSCIOUS IN PLATO AND ARISTOTLE

The history of emopoesis in Greek philosophy is complex, as it dates back even to mythologies such as that of Apollo and Dionysus, which was a narrative of two Gods inserted into a dynamic that contrasted dualities between day and night, harmony and disharmony, wisdom and subversion, among others. But for the Greeks like Plato, the entities, as well as being dual, could also be complementary, as highlighted in *Phaedrus*, in the myth of the charioteer, in which the human soul is composed of a white horse that designates *an Apollonian* element of the soul, that is, reason - to the extent that intellect is what distinguishes man from a beast - which seeks perfection, elevation, luminosity and truth, while the black horse disrupts Apollonian reason: the overwhelming, unbridled and furious *Dionysian* impulse (OLIVEIRA, 2012). The fact that the charioteer tries to control both horses, which are going in opposite directions, is related to a tripartite conception of the soul, since the charioteer is the third element in the plot and, as a background figure, there is a dualism between the two horses.

In *Republic VII,* the well-known Socratic dialogue of the Allegory of the Cave is one of the main references in Plato's works on the representations of *logos* and *pathos* with knowledge of reality. This well-known dialogue concerns men who have always lived as prisoners in a cave and have ended up seeing a back wall that is illuminated by the light of a fire, and that casts shadows of people, animals and other objects. When the prisoner comes out of the cave, he realizes that these projections are only ghostly, which from a philosophical point of view is a passage from the sensible world to the intelligible[4] . Although Plato was Aristotle's forerunner in some respects when it came to discussing the rational and irrational aspects of the *psyche,* in the Allegory of the Cave, in *Republica*, it is possible to see a hybrid between the knowable world - the *logos*, and the sensible world which is represented by *pathos* (passion) which also acts on the plane of distorted ideas about the cave and its intrinsic reality, in order to consequently know the truth. It should be added, however, that the sensitive part of the irascible *(thumikon)* soul, so to speak, is not just a matter of overshadowing reason, because without this intermediary part of the soul it is not possible to teach virtue, since merely knowing the means to educate man would be unscathed, because the irascible component needs to be mobilized by the *logos* in order to give power to the deliberation of educating the soul in its entirety. This brief summary of the dynamics between reason and emotion in Plato elucidates the dilemmas that man has in understanding and acting in accordance with his conflictive nature. However, in Aristotelian doctrine, the resolution of the conflicts of the soul does not consist of resolving any

4 The dialogue of the allegory of the cave was summarized in the dissertation, based on Book VII of the *Republic* (PLATO, 1997).

manifestations of the emotional field, since it is reason itself that operates within the emogogues to empower the deliberations that involve man's actions. It's enough to remember that, in Aristotelian philosophy, the desiderative part of the soul is the one capable of obeying reason, while the vegetative part is situated only in the irrational register. Perhaps the most complex metaphysics in ancient philosophy, Aristotle also addresses the mental aspects of the human being. The aim of this work will be to look at a metaphysics that comes close to Freud's metapsychology: that of the German philosopher Schopenhauer.

4 ENCOUNTERS AND DISAGREEMENTS BETWEEN THE SCHOPENHAUERIAN METAPHYSICAL SYSTEM AND FREUDIAN METAPSYCHOLOGY

With the publication of the metapsychological articles, Freud began to work on the psyche from a new perspective within his psychoanalytic theory, thus breaking with the classical psychology of his time. Freud restructured his theory to the extent that the information obtained through clinical material was reformulating his concepts for their practical foundation. Metapsychology, this new system within psychoanalysis, was named in this way by Freud because its use was intended to go beyond the psychology of his time, and the prefix *meta* refers precisely to this. The content of this prefix found in Freud's works occupies a certain configuration on a plane[5] of metaphysics, but refers to other regions and aims to solve different problems.

Psychoanalytic theory seeks to solve a problem in the empirical study and treatment of neuroses. Metapsychology is then formulated with the aim of researching and describing the disturbances in conscious psychic life observed in clinical practice (LOPARIC, 2001). Based on these observations, Freud used his interpretative method to unveil the unconscious contents.

For Birman (2003), it was through metapsychology that the fundamental problematic of psychoanalysis was transposed into philosophy. This system consisted of three concepts (the *topical, the dynamic and the economic)* whose function was to explain

[5] It is in the territory of the concept that the bridges for conceptual construction are relocated.

mental phenomena and the psychic places in which they occurred.

The topical point of view consists of outlining the psychic registers in which that experience would be taking place and what kind of representation would be in evidence. In this configuration, the psyche would be like an apparatus, it would be possible to visualize it and picture it as if it were a telescope, a microscope or an object with similar characteristics, thus creating the possibility of assimilating and differentiating the psychic instances that make up this apparatus, never relating it to any anatomical region. The dynamic refers to the pulses in conflict, they are the motor forces that originate the functioning of psychic life; the economic is the presupposition of a libidinal energy that is understood in its quantitative form, which moves the pulses and the investments in the object of desire (FULGENCIO, 2003). Regarding the difference between the topical and dynamic conceptions of the unconscious, the topical point of view was used in Freud's first explanation of repression, while in the dynamic perspective, Freud did not aim for a mechanical separation between the unconscious, preconscious and conscious, but in the dynamic point of view - which underpinned Freudian metapsychology - the impulses move in psychic bodies that are represented by the id, ego and superego. In this way, metapsychology is described as an open knowledge that is restructured according to clinical results, in which concepts have the function of structuring psychoanalysis; whereas Schopenhauer's proposal was to develop a philosophy to unveil the enigma of the universe based on will and representation.

Another methodological difference from metapsychology was that Schopenhauer's metaphysics was not part of a positivist context like Freud's, but it still operated within Freud's discourse, helping him to develop concepts that dealt with aspects of the unconscious. Even though Schopenhauer verified phenomena through experience, in order to arrive at knowledge of the thing itself, it was necessary to formulate metaphysical concepts that would allow us to understand how the objectification of the notion of madness would occur from a mental perspective, from an individual's perspective. In his main work, *The World as Will and Representation*, Schopenhauer goes through various branches of knowledge in order to develop the concept of will, which relates to a metaphysical root of the world.

When discussing the question of will, it can be seen that Schopenhauer conceives of it as the thing itself, representing the essence underlying the world. As a result, the world of representations or phenomena can simultaneously be considered as will. The human will is the clearest phenomenon of the will *(Wille),* but in the human will there is participation of the intellect. Schopenhauer will work these two instances into a duality between will and intellect, where the conscious and rational intellect is subordinated to an unconscious and volitional will (SCHOPENHAUER, 2004).

Although Freud's metapsychology and Schopenhauer's metaphysics correspond in some respects, the territory in which the concepts are found in the postulates of both authors occupies different spaces and horizons within their systems. But some Schopenhauerian concepts served as Freud's potency for his constant reinventions. For Raikovic (1996), Schopenhauer "clothed his intuition in a system [...] [*and*], as a result, there is a solution of continuity between the idea and the systematics that we do not find in other post-Kantians. One can incorporate into this statement a certain discontinuity in the spaces occupied by Freud-Schopenhauer's systems, but on the other hand, there is continuity between their ideas. Schopenhauer's experimentalism regarding the etiology of madness complemented the concept of repression, as Freud grasped the necessary components to reinvent this concept. However, both concepts occupy spaces that encompass different systems, in which they aim to take the problem in different directions, since their ideas complement each other, but their systems keep them apart.

For Loparic (2001), the theoretical contribution of the speculative method is not Freud's part of a science of the *nature of* the psyche and the psyche, nor is it the ultimate *foundation of* psychoanalysis, rather, it functions as a speculative "superstructure" which is a set of "conventions" - "auxiliary constructions" coupled together for the purpose of their methodological and heuristic use in the organization of material from the clinic ("empirical"), in the search for new clinical results. On the other hand, Schopenhauer's metaphysical concepts are not used as conventions, with the concepts of will and madness, because Schopenhauer aimed to gather prepositions to solidify his concepts, to increase their consistency and strengthen them through analogies, based on his empirical observations.

Freudian speculation aims to organize his empirical materials in search of new psychoanalytic results, with the help of his interpretative method. The direction of Schopenhauerian speculation is to grasp the essence of reality intuitively in order to unveil it with the help of abstract representations.

They are also speculative, since they involve an essentialism around the rules that govern the universe and the volitional flows common to all categories of thing, in which "the essence of the world is the true substratum of phenomena, that which is freed from all change and is therefore known as the same truth for all times, in a word, the ideas, which constitute the immediate and adequate objectivity of the thing itself" (SCHOPENHAUER, 2004). Schopenhauer's intuition is therefore confined to the infrastructure of his system of thought.

The territory[6] that speculation occupies within Freud-Schopenhauer's conceptual structures sets them apart, even though they both speculate, but the way in which these speculations are problematized lead them in different directions. In Freud, its use is only justified because it helps to organize empirical data, not because it necessarily corresponds to a possible element of the phenomena (FULGENCIO, 2003). In Schopenhauer's view of intuitive representation: "it comprises the entire visible world, or experience in general, with the conditions that make it possible (SCHOPENHAUER, 2004). Therefore, unlike Freud, Schopenhauerian speculation aims to grasp and unveil the essence of empirical reality.

Even if this schematic separation between their thinking is

[6] And the possibility of orienting thought.

plausible, it is possible to complicate the relationship between them a little more - and for the sake of this relationship. In fact, the concepts postulated by Freud carry with them sediments of other concepts that pursued other goals. These conceptual components of metaphysics served as elements that allowed Freud to architect his metapsychology with the abstraction and depth that would take him beyond the information obtained from empirical data, thus allowing him to develop the three points of view: *topical, economic and dynamic* in line with the preponderant intensity that the unconscious exerts over consciousness.

Having seen some of the disagreements and encounters between Schopenhauer's and Freud's systems, we are now in a position to delve deeper into some of the elements highlighted so far. Therefore, in the course of the research, repression will be problematized by specifying the three points of view in metapsychology, taking into account that each point of view was used by Freud himself, only in the situations in which they were necessary:

It won't be out of place to give a special name to this global way of considering our subject, because it is the consummation of psychoanalytic research. I propose that when we have succeeded in describing a psychic process in its dynamic, topographical and economic aspects, we refer to it as a metapsychological presentation. We should state straight away that in the present state of our knowledge there are only a few points at which this task will be successful (FREUD, 1996).

5 SCHOPENHAUER'S EMPIRICAL EXPERIENCE IN THE *CHARITE* HOSPITAL AS A BASIS FOR CREATING THE CONCEPT OF MADNESS

Initially, Schopenhauer's idea of madness seems to have its roots only in philosophical speculation, as it is not a concise and properly systematized theory. However, from the historical documents recovered by Zentner, it was possible to see that the factor that contributed to Schopenhauer's thinking on madness was his empirical experience, when he came into contact with patients in the psychiatric ward of the Charite hospital in Berlin, which Schopenhauer visited constantly in 1811 (ROTHE-NEVES, 2002). In *The World as Will and Representation,* we can find indications of Schopenhauer's contact with patients at the Charite hospital when he states:

> I often visited homes for the insane and found them to be of unquestionable value; their genius manifested itself distinctly through their madness had remained completely dominant (SCHOPENHAUER, 2004).

Aiming to investigate the problem of sanity and illness in the individual, in the fall of 1809, as soon as he was able, Schopenhauer chose to study medicine at the Faculty of Medicine in Gottingen and after three or four months, despite his preference for medicine, he left that faculty, because he didn't like Enlightenment organicism, and because he wanted to research philosophy; therefore, he thought he should become a philosopher. Disillusioned with Fitche's lectures, which expressed an idealistic proposal about the mental field, Schopenhauer ended up deciding to do his own research in solitude and freedom, but not locked in his own room, but in direct contact with subjects (IANNACO, 1998).

The idealistic and abstract play on words that do not relate the thing to reality, and materialistic optimism, were not realistic methods for Schopenhauer, as he recognizes:

> In particular, I'm glad that I was used to it so early on (...) that I'm not content with simply naming things and prefer, over the sea of words, the awareness born of observation. For this reason, I never ran the risk of taking words for things (SCHOPENHAUER, 2004, p. 13).

6 THE SCHOPENHAUERIAN ETIOLOGY OF MADNESS AS ONE OF THE ELEMENTS IN THE CO-CREATION OF THE CONCEPT OF REPRESSION

One of the first references to the similarities between Freud's text and Schopenhauer's was made in 1926 in an article written by Otto Juliusberger, a Berlin doctor who was a member of one of the many Schopenhauerian societies present at the time. Juliusberger argued that Freud used themes and thoughts already anticipated in Schopenhauer's works in his psychoanalytic discourse (RAIKOVIC, 1996). The readings carried out so far indicate that Zentner also holds the opinion that Schopenhauer anticipated the Freudian theory of repression, and even analyzes this anticipation as a "plagiarism" of Freud (ZENTNER, 1995).

Freud saw this similarity as a mere coincidence, even when Otto Rank reminded him that Schopenhauer had an explanation for madness in *The World as Will and Representation.* Freud claims that he didn't know the works of this philosopher when he was working on his theory of repression. He also states that "the theory of repression undoubtedly occurred to me independently of any other source" (FREUD, 1996). Rank added that Freud had also deprived himself of the great pleasure of reading Nietzsche.

In *The World as Will and Representation,* Schopenhauer discusses the idea that madness emanates from a need to forget and dissolve conscious records of adjacent painful experiences of reality, such as "violent moral pains" and "terrible events" (SCHOPENHAUER, 2004). For Schopenhauer (2004), the mechanism of madness arises when an extremely arduous and distressing event for the individual reaches their threshold of tolerance and, in response, their nature resorts to madness as a "last resort" to end this pain. Thus "the tortured spirit breaks, as it were, the thread of its memory" (SCHOPENHAUER, 2004), allowing the individual to temporarily recover their mental integrity. This amnesia stems from a conflict between the Will and the Intellect and, if some content is painful for the Will, it prevents the Intellect from becoming aware of it. Raikovic (1996) points out that the defensive strategy of the psychic apparatus requires a higher kind of intelligence, since the past that has been forgotten is an artifice with the function of protecting what according to this "intelligence" would be in danger.

The function of madness would functionally play a diminishing role in conflicts analogous to those postulated by Freud. Thus, symptomatically, the illness would act through a mental need to be able to forget these painful memories, with the aim of eliminating anguish and reducing displeasure. For Raikovic (1996), the purpose of this mechanism was to make representations more bearable; once these representations were free to surface, as they are, in consciousness, they would pose a danger to individual maintenance, which minimally requires internal cohesion, even at the cost of ignorance.

For Freud, "the essence of repression consists simply in removing something from the conscious, keeping it at a distance" *(*FREUD, 1996). But if we deal with a concept from a perspective of description and analysis that is not focused on its essence, its understanding would not encompass its many facets, the paths it has traveled throughout its history, its process of creation while it was being constituted, and its becoming. Thinking about repression from various perspectives, Freud says that "we must be prepared to encounter a similar multiplicity of mechanisms of eruption (or symptom formation), and we can already begin to suspect that it will not be possible to trace all these multiplicities back to the developmental history of the libido alone" (FREUD, 1996).

Schopenhauer's metaphysics permeated the concept of repression in some initial aspects of its elaboration, but with Freud's constant reformulations of this concept, the[7] intensive immanence of repression gained in volume, as it began to interact with a greater number of concepts within psychoanalysis, causing the relapse of repression to occur through pulses, objects, structures and other mechanisms of the psyche. This is precisely what characterizes the inner solidity of the concept, or in Deleuze's words, its endo-consistency (DELEUZE, 1992).

Each distinct component of repression is made up of elements that make its components indiscernible from one another; the concept of repression is partly neighboring with other concepts. The concept doesn't have just one component, even the original concept, by which a philosophy "begins", has several sediments, since it's not clear that philosophy should begin and that, if it proclaims one, it should add a point of view or a reason to it (DELEUZE, 1992). The question of madness in Schopenhauer

[7] Immanence refers to its links and conjunctions with other concepts that allow meaning to emerge.

in relation to psychopathology. For these authors, Schopenhauer understands madness to mean what we currently call psychosis or severe affective disorder, in which case madness does not affect all mental capacities.

However, there are countless texts that deal with the issue of madness, with descriptions, facts, considerations and classifications, but as Schopenhauer says: "but I have never found a clear and satisfactory explanation of the intrinsic nature of madness, of what it is and how it differs from sanity (SCHOPENHAUER, 2004).

For Schopenhauer (2004), the conversion of representations into a symptomatology presented in the form of illness would be a reaction to preserve individuality. In the Freudian view, defense mechanisms are used as a natural response of the psychic structure to eliminate such anguish. This reaction could emerge through a primary gain, where the reduction of tension and conflict would occur through a neurotic or hysterical illness. This whole process, which has its key in repression[8] , occurs when a representative content from the conscious is transferred to the unconscious, and as a result becomes a pathology.

The concept of madness, like repression, unfolded through observations of subjects whose life experiences gave them a unique subjectivity. This subjectivity was interpreted as an illness for the time, and the study was aimed at understanding the processes that were responsible for the formation of a symptom.

---

[8] LAPLANCHE, J and PONTALIS, L. *Vocabulario da Psicanalise.* Trad. Pedro Tamen. Sao Paulo: Martins Fontes, 1992.

Talking about the states of the individual's maintenance leads us to a concept that goes back to the genesis of this individuality: the individual is not formed forever. As such, the individual is undergoing different stages of realization, the pathology of which, in its multiplicity, fails to take into account what could be the solutions to mask a possible danger of "deindividuation" (RAIKOVIC, 1996).

Both in the etiology of madness and in repression, the events that trigger the activation of both mechanisms, which aim to recover the integrity of the self, involve an activation through a traumatic situation, event or idea. So let's try to establish the correspondence between the idea of trauma and the etiology of madness and repression.

In the Freudian conception, trauma is the result of the failure of mechanisms whose function is to protect the apparatus from very intense excitations. For Freud (1996), the "great isolated trauma is generally replaced by a series of smaller traumas which are interrelated because of their similarity or because they form part of a painful history". When repression is activated, this mobilization also occurs through a kind of micro-trauma. There is a greater influx of stimuli: a lot of excitement enters the psychic apparatus in a given time and cannot be controlled; traumatic experiences are part of this order (FENICHEL, 1969). In the psychic apparatus in its economic dimension, trauma is constituted by a large amount of inactivated drive, which exceeds the containment capacity of the systems of psychic representation. Freud's explanation of the functioning of this psychic system is greater than

Schopenhauer's here.

Trauma involves pain suffered by the individual in the face of an event. Freud characterized pain as an eruption of an intense volume of quantities directed at the memory system, as a result of the failure of the devices that would protect the apparatus against very strong exogenous quantities (CAROPRESO, 2006).

In the mechanism of madness, according to Schopenhauer, a trauma of great intensity causes the intolerable and impossible forces of admitting oneself to move these chains of representations to another non-conscious structure. With regard to the topographical perspective of psychic acts and the transposition of chains of representations, when this act (an idea) is moved from the unconscious to the conscious system, this change unfolds in a new register, a second register that can be found in a new psychic location, momentarily, to the original unconscious register. Therefore, this idea is present in the psyche in more than one register, and situated in more than one region of the mental mechanism. In the etiology of madness, what can be observed are different ideas in different instances, according to the analysis of this passage:

> I suppose that a madman evokes a scene from the past and gives it all the vividness of a truly present scene: there are gaps in this memory; the madman fills them with fictions; these fictions can always be the same and become fixed ideas or they can change every time, like ephemeral accidents; in the first case, it is monomania, melancholia; in the second case, dementia (SCHOPENHAUER, 2004).

When a representation of the past is evoked by the madman, his memory, which makes up a second region that is not part of the present conscious state, distorts the original idea from the first region, which means that the first record of the original representation is no longer the same, because it has been replaced by a fiction, it has become a fixed idea. The repressed material, in Freud-Schopenhauer's conception, has not been erased, it is kept in a non-conscious partition, the psychic content has been temporarily moved, and this content may return in another substitute form or a symptom may emerge.

The path of the force that was repressed in Freud-Schopenhauer has characteristics in common, because when a process of an initial idea generates a different one, we know that this transmutation was only possible through the forces that went from the unconscious to the conscious.

With regard to Freud's earlier description of repression. As a result of this, the founding concept of psychoanalysis, repression, emerged; its final determinant was always one of Freud's doubts; the ultimate determinant of repression, which was conscious, was once unconscious, or even this process could be linked to both structures.

Both Freud and Schopenhauer work with repression by specifying fantasy and substitutive symptoms, even using the same term. From a metapsychological perspective, the structuring of the concept of defense is linked to a hypothesis about mental functioning, which is that of a representational perspective of the psyche. Its dynamics are based on an energetic investment, the energy of the forces behind mental representations is displaceable and impulses with a greater amount of energy are more difficult to repress than those with a lower amount of energy, but they can be repressed if the opposing forces are equivalent in terms of the amount of energy. For Fenichel (1969), the amount of excitation that can be supported without discharge is an economic problem, because there is an exchange of mental energy, an economic distribution of energy between input, consumption and output.

In the case of the etiology of madness, it is presented in a more rudimentary way[9] than the theory of repression. The representations to which Schopenhauer referred when problematizing the question of madness do not have a quantitative energetic idea and the representation in madness moves from one particular mental region to another, neither involving an energetic nor an economic issue. This representation is displaced to the extent that the intellect, by force of will, can no longer support this representation; its displacement circumscribes the representation itself; it is not a question of its energetic distribution, but of a force that aims to safeguard the integrity of the Self.

In his main work *The World as Will and Representation*, Schopenhauer uses his knowledge, which spans various fields of knowledge, to develop the concept of the metaphysical root of the world, the will. In discussing the question of the will, we can see that Schopenhauer conceives of it as the thing itself, representing the underlying essence of the world. Consequently,

[9] It has a relatively smaller number of components compared to countersinking. Filling brings with it greater internal inseparability of the communication zones.

the world of representations or phenomena can be considered as will.

The human will is the clearest phenomenon of the will *(Wille),* but in the human will there is participation of the intellect. Schopenhauer would draw a parallel between will and intellect, where the conscious and rational intellect is subordinate to an unconscious and volitional will. Also sharing this view in its dual aspect[10] , Freud would transcribe this duality into conscious-unconscious, an opposition between the knowable and unknowable. Both authors postulate in their theories instances that describe the set of contents that do not participate in the field composed of consciousness. Freud calls this instance the Unconscious, which is energized by a drive, while Schopenhauer calls this same instance the Will.

In this sense, the formation of an unconscious process postulated by Schopenhauer-Freud presupposes a general theory of human nature, in which desires, the search for pleasure, play a primary role, and the perception of reality a secondary role (ZENTNER, 1995).

Furthermore, Schopenhauer, in this case in agreement with Kant, maintains that "the will is the thing in itself, foreign to time"[11] . This Kantian proposition maintains that space, time and causality do not belong to the thing itself, but are only forms of knowledge, which leads us to think that these principles were possibly echoed in the formulation of the Freudian unconscious

---

[10] The duality is most evident in the "first hypothesis, the topographical one, which is closely linked to that of a topographical separation of the *Ics. and CS.* systems, and also to the possibility that an idea can exist simultaneously in two places in the mental mechanism". (Freud, 1969, p.181.vol XIV).

[11] SCHOPENHAUER, A. op. cit.

(SCHOPENHAUER, 2004).

In contrast to the image of a rhizomatic structure of thought, the root that emerges from the construction of the meaning of the concept of will, has as its starting point the intuition[12] , and for its solidity as a concept, Schopenhauer uses reasoning *per analogiam.* To begin with, the aim of this reasoning is to verify the omnipresence of the will in the phenomenal world. To do this, Schopenhauer uses explanations that figure the will in its empirical form and its objectification among plant media, physical phenomena, art and any other identifiable means.

Schopenhauer therefore starts from the particular in order to define a general status, an absolute concept. And that the world of representation refers to a specific type of sedentary distribution, which divides or shares the distributed in order to give "everyone" their fixed share (DELEUZE, 2006). The concept of will, while it was being constituted, led Schopenhauer to attach one example of will to another, bringing together its sediments to form a whole and simultaneously each sediment having its own part in this whole. In this way, the will nourishes a character of uniqueness, which leads us to conclude that Schopenhauer probably aimed to make the will an infinite concept in all its parts, and from this infinity, to prove its elementarity. [13]

Let's take a closer look at some examples in which

[12] An intuitive philosophical speculation can be the initial step and serve as inspiration for empirically testable hypotheses.

[13] "It is not in the manner of an object, whose unity is only recognized by opposition to possible plurality; nor is it in the manner of a concept of unity, which exists only by abstraction from plurality". (SCHOPENHAUER, 2004). "Its unity must be recognized by the aspect of intimate kinship that all its manifestations have" (SCHOPENHAUER, 2004).

Schopenhauer describes the will in the empirical world through his reasoning *per analogiam:*

If we look closely, if we see the powerful, irresistible impetus with which the waters rush into the depths, the tenacity with which the magnet always turns towards the north pole, the attraction it exerts on iron, the violence that grows with obstacles, like human desires; if we consider the speed with which crystallization takes place, the regularity of crystals, which results only from a movement in different directions that is suddenly stopped and subjected, in its solidification, to strict laws; if we observe the discernment with which bodies deprived of the lakes of solidity and set free in the fluid state seek each other or avoid each other, unite or separate; and, finally, if we notice how a weight that our body prevents from being attracted to the center of the earth continuously compresses and weighs on this body, according to the law of attraction (SCHOPENHAUER, 2004).

Among these examples described by Schopenhauer that can be visualized in nature, and which move inorganic bodies, we find in the midst of these observations, different allegations based on analogies that go from physical principles to human desire. Deleuze argues that the fundamental aspect of analogy is that it encompasses a certain permissiveness, even with its generic, specific and natural differences (DELEUZE, 2006).

Although there is an enormous distance, and even an apparent opposition between the phenomena of the inorganic world and the most intimate will of our essence, this is fundamentally due to the determined character of the one and the apparent free will of the other, since in man individuality stands out powerfully, each person has their own character; This is why the same cause does not have the same effect on everyone, among countless circumstances that encompass a person's wide range of knowledge and which remain unknown to others, and modify their action; (SCHOPENHAUER, 2004). The difference between consciousnesses, then, is due to the distinction and graduation between each person's knowledge and representation.

Will is omnipresent in the world, but its acts of objectification differ radically in intensity. At the lowest level of will, we find the manifestations of all inorganic nature; these are the first forces that physics and chemistry have to unveil and know their laws. To the extent that it increases in intensity, the will also begins to act in the plant kingdom, where its connection with phenomena is no longer a cause, but an excitation (SCHOPENHAUER, 2004).

The most explicit phenomenon of the will is found in humans, where representation and intellect come into play, which differs from all other means in which the will is actualized. It is in the human being that the power of representation has the highest degree of perfection, it is capable of intuitive, abstract and rational representations. In *Justification of the Concept of the Unconscious,* Freud seems to refer to Schopenhauer when he discusses the question of consciousness in inanimate objects, but in his words:

This inference[14] (or this identification) was previously extended by the ego to other human beings, animals, plants, inanimate objects and the world in general, and proved useful while its similarity to the individual ego was overwhelming; however, it became less trustworthy as the difference between the ego and these 'others' increased. Today, our critical judgment is already

[14] By inference, Freud means "Consciousness makes each of us aware only of our own mental states; that other people also possess a consciousness and a deduction which we infer by analogy from their observable statements and actions, so that their conduct becomes intelligible to us". *(*FREUD, 1969).

casting doubt on the question of the existence of consciousness in animals; we refuse to admit it in plants and regard the supposition of its existence in inanimate things as mysticism (FREUD, 1969).

Like Schopenhauer, Freud used an analogical inference that differs from Schopenhauer's, since he didn't spread a possible consciousness or unconsciousness in animals, plants and other inanimate beings. His deductive foundation was focused on a clinical context, touching on the human psyche.

Raikovic (1996) argues that Freud used the same analogical reasoning, seeking a similar end to Schopenhauer, striving to show that the individual psyche has the same foundation, the unconscious, and in order to demonstrate the existence of the same unconscious in each individual, in each psychic apparatus, it is first necessary to have proved the existence of a consciousness in each individual[15] . However, even though Freud recognized the similarities between his theories and those of Schopenhauer, he always gave priority to scientific work and clinical observation when formulating his discoveries (CACCIOLA, 1991).

We agree on the structure of thought *per analogiam* used by both authors, but let's also add that due to the empiricism present in the psychoanalytic system, Freud used other techniques[16] to incorporate his concept of the unconscious, such as failed acts, dreams and others, which were duly systematized in order to apply them strictly in the clinical field. It is possible to

---

[15] "The unconscious is *conceivable* only and exclusively in terms accessible to the light of consciousness" (LOPARIC, 2001).

[16] "The study of ramblings, when the patient is subject to psychoanalytic rules, is not the only technical resource for probing the unconscious. Two other processes serve the same purpose: the interpretation of dreams and the study of lapses and casual acts." (FREUD, 1970).

reiterate that Freud did not aim for a *complete reduction of* philosophy to psychoanalysis, as he admitted the existence of conceptual problems that his science poses, but which cannot be solved alone (LOPARIC).

Firstly, the process of constructing the concept of the unconscious is complemented by the concept of the will. In this fusion of interdisciplinary knowledge, Schopenhauer's metaphysics served as a foundation that enabled Freud to construct his concept of the unconscious, even though it occupies different spaces and has different objectives.

It was in his personal relationship with the inmates of *Charite* that Schopenhauer developed a conviction about the etiology of madness, a theory of forgetfulness (das *Vergessen).* It would become a pillar for the construction of an original and more general metaphysical conception that he would have presented in the work he was thinking about and preparing, even before he had written his graduation dissertation *On the Fourfold Root of the Principle of Sufficient Reason*[17] , and which would have been completed in 1918, five years later, with the title *The World as Will and Representation,* a book for the dissemination of which he would later have given greater importance and of which very few copies were sold (IANNACO, 1998).

Now we have the etiology of madness, a concept of forgetfulness (*Vergessen*), whose endo-consistency created possibilities for another concept to emerge, the will. In Freud, within his own system, the agency is similar, since the concept

[17] A. Schopenhauer, *Uber die vierfache Wurzel des Satzes vom zureichenden Grunde*, Weimar, 1813 (IANNACO, 1998).

of the unconscious[18] began with the theory of repression[19] . Internally, its development took place through psychoanalytic techniques, through the reports of his patients and the analysis of his own unconscious.

The inseparability of the internal zones of communication that have been dealt with so far concerns the corresponding quadrangle of the theory of forgetting[20] - will and repression - unconscious. But all this configuration and combination between one concept and another, in particular, can be redefined and reordered by other combinations, but with this recombination, its exo- consistency, would bring the possibility of articulation between the concepts on different planes of immanence. Metaphysics and psychoanalysis are distinct systems, but their concepts can be co-created by the continuity between their ideas, even if they aim to solve other problems and occupy other territories.

The metaphysical system and psychoanalysis can work with the question of concepts that involve the whole, making it infinite, in order to clarify this question. Schopenhauer's will has a tendency towards the infinite, which according to Deleuze is embedded in reasoning by analogy. Let's look at an example taken from Schopenhauer himself:

In order to manifest itself in all its value, the idea of man needed not to be expressed alone and disconnected, but had to be accompanied by the descending series of degrees through all forms, passing through the plant kingdom to inorganic matter:

---

[18] We recognize that the *Ics.* does not coincide with the repressed; it is still true that everything that is repressed *is Ics.*, but not everything that is *Ics.* is repressed (FREUD, 1987).

[19] We thus obtain our concept of the unconscious from the theory of repression (FREUD, 1987).

[20] It was developed through the etiology of madness.

they form a whole and come together for the complete objectification of the will; the idea of man presupposes them, just as the flowers presuppose the leaves of the tree, the branches, the trunk and the root: they form a pyramid of which man is the top (SCHOPENHAUER, 2004).

The will in the world has no beginning or end; it is one, indivisible and omnipresent. The possible forms of objectification of the will compel only it, it is not possible to split the human will, or any other substantiation of the will, from itself.

as a whole, it is the ulterior truth behind empirical phenomena.

Although man occupies the top of the pyramid, he only has the capacity to presuppose the existence of will, but it has no beginning or end, it is the thing itself that is always present. Its relative minimum or maximum could be understood as the variation of the degrees and forms of its objectivity, but in order to think of its potency, it is first necessary to think of it as a whole in order to be able to picture the image of the will in thought.

The unconscious is an insoluble structure, preponderant over the others, occupying the highest degree of interference and determinism in the psychic apparatus. It is universal in the sense that in order to assume the existence of an unconscious in each individual, it is necessary to have proven the existence of a consciousness in each individual: "a reasoning which, to paraphrase Schopenhauer, he calls 'inference *per analogiam',* which allows him to go from recognizing the existence of his own consciousness to recognizing a consciousness in any individual being" (RAIKOVIC, 1996). (RAIKOVIC, 1996).The unconscious only circumscribes psychic phenomena, Freud's observation can be easily understood: our unconscious is an "object" in its essence, different from the physical world, which is only accessible in perception and remains, as a thing in itself, unknowable, due to its subjective conditioning."[21] (LOPARIC, 2001). In the following, points of encounter and disagreement between Freud and Schopenhauer will be exposed, implying conceptions of the human being that refer to the paradigm of psychic determinism.

---

[21] "Psychoanalysis, Freud adds, makes the point that the psychic itself, like the physical, need not be as it appears to us. Even so, Freud suggests somewhat enigmatically at the end of the text, psychic ("inner") reality would be less unknowable than physical ("outer") reality" (LOPARIC, 2001).

7 THE WILL AND THE UNCONSCIOUS AS FURTHER DETERMINING AGENTS IN MENTAL PROCESSES

Schopenhauer breaks with the Cartesian paradigm by developing the idea that free will and the choices of each individual are not the responsibility of the conscience.[22] In other words, it's not up to them to give the final verdict. In fact, reason can do little to deal with the determinants of acts that are enclosed in a will. The only thing that is really free is the driving force behind the motivations, i.e. the will, but only the will itself, isolated from the phenomena of the empirical world, as opposed to representation. The following hierarchy of psychological functions applies to this determination: "The known mind is already composed: it is the link between desire and the *nous*, intellect. This intellect is secondary, and the *posteriorius* of the organism and conditioned as a simple function of the brain. Desire in turn is primary, and the *prius* of the organism is conditioned by it" (ZENTNER, 1995).

For Freud, the topographical assumption regarding the relationship between the unconscious and the conscious strictly refers to a topographical separation between the *Ics. and Cs.* systems, and it is also possible for an idea to exist simultaneously in two places in the mental mechanism (Freud, 1974). Based on these statements by Freud and Schopenhauer, regarding the confluence or non-confluence between the different psychic instances or forces that determine mental processes, we have seen that for Schopenhauer-Freud in his topographical perspective there is a dual separation between

[22] The Cartesian notion of consciousness.

the unconscious and conscious, one primary and the other secondary.

However, it should be noted that the unconscious and the conscious can simultaneously harbor the same idea or thought shared by both structures. With the second topic, the interlocution of the unconscious with structures such as the id, ego and superego becomes greater, and the schism between consciousness and unconsciousness becomes less evident. The superego is unable to obey most of the demands made by the impulses coming from the id, but these structures are complementary, one does not cancel out the other, although this relationship is predominantly conflictual.

In Schopenhauer's view, the will starts exclusively from the will, its only primordial source. The intellect can also become aware of this will, but it doesn't have the power to make decisions, it can't modify a will in its favor. The will converges with the intellect, but desires and volitions have always come from the will.

The ideas and images of the intellect have the possibility of setting the will in motion, however, in this affectation of the will, the rational contents are sometimes not openly perceived and the mutation of the intellectual component into the volitional component is very quick, for the immediate perception of the fact (CACCIOLA, 1991).

In Schopenhauer's metaphysics, every act can be realized by a decision of the will, but first there must be a need or motive, which acts as the starting point for this act that is in potency. These acts of the will always have an externalized foundation of their own. In their motives, they determine "the will *at such and such a time, in such and such a place, in such and such a circumstance*; and not the will in general, *or its content"* (SCHOPENHAUER, 2004). Therefore, for an act to be consolidated, these actions will always be governed according to the principle of causality, the objectification of the will in its empirical reality, as a phenomenon, will always have a cause as the triggering principle for its effect.

In his first texts, Freud had a strong conviction that causalist thinking and its phenomena could be investigated by the natural sciences, which could also be applied to psychic phenomena. Initially, Freud looked exclusively for a single trauma in the lives of hysterics that could explain their pathology, and by bringing this memory to consciousness, it would be possible to cure the illness.

Later on, we will see Freud's understanding that the same effect can have several causes, and that there are many factors in a person's life that contribute to structuring their psyche in a certain way. This understanding of multiple causes makes the analyst's task of uncovering the construction of an underlying meaning even more complex. Thus, there is nothing meaningless, arbitrary or causal in psychic appearances, but there are *multiple* causes for the same effect (FREUD, 1970).

Through the psychoanalytic clinic developed by Freud, it was possible to problematize psychic determinism involving its various causes and possible effects. For Loparic (2001), the main meaning of the term "dynamic" is causal: "According to Freud, the proof of the existence of the dynamic unconscious lies in the possibility of providing dynamic (causal) explanations for the existence of symptoms". In order to uncover the determinants of the psyche, psychoanalytic techniques are used, such as interpretations, failed acts and dreams, which are working materials for the analyst to access unconscious formations and create new paths and possibilities with the patient.

But what could be a possible solution to escape Freud and Schopenhauer's psychic determinism? First of all, every solution refers to a problematic, that is, the construction of a unified systematic field that directs and submits research or interrogations in such a way that the answers form precise cases of solution (DELEUZE, 2006).

As a solution to minimize this psychic determinism, Freudian psychoanalysis shows us a way out. Nothing in the mind happens at random, each psychic occurrence is determined by other antecedents, and the causes are not only linear since many of them can produce the same effect, the psychoanalyst will create new forms for the patient, rescue his speech and connect it with the other speech, In this way we can consider the psychic apparatus as always accessible to re-significations, breaking away from a linear determinism, finding marks available for re-symbolization, expanding new horizons, because the trauma is not something that is solidified, tied up in the past, but something that did not find a possibility of symbolization at the time of its inscription.

Firstly, Schopenhauer's model should also serve to represent and clarify observations about psychic formations, processes and conflicts (ZENTNER, 1995). In his metaphysics, only the will in itself is free. One of the possible ways of escaping psychic determinism is partly conditional on renouncing any need. In this abnegation, the will would have no determination, either by a reason or a cause, the volitions would emerge randomly, reaching an undifferentiated freedom.

For the author, the only way out of the freedom of the will is abnegation, which is capable of the very essence suppressing itself: that is the true, the only way in which freedom of the will can emerge (SCHOPENHAUER, 2004). A positive thought of philosophy that only externalizes in a negative way, is the negation of the will [sic..], what is called ecstasy, rapture, enlightenment, union with God etc. These states are not knowledge, because they no longer have the form of object and subject, they belong only to personal experience; it is impractical to communicate their idea externally to others (SCHOPENHAUER, 2004).

The search for a transcendent state[23] is always renouncing desires and living cautiously. In order to tread this path of caution, it is first necessary to grasp this ascetic knowledge through the intellect, although Schopenhauer does not suggest using his philosophy for everyday practice. The denial of desires and the renunciation of volitions are part of the metaphysical realm. Freedom is not seen as the realization of various acts in conjunction with individual decisions and choices, but rather as the denial of such acts that could make the objectification of the

[23] "Transcendent in no way means that the faculty addresses itself to objects situated outside the world, but, on the contrary, that it apprehends in the world what concerns it exclusively and which gives it birth in the world" (DELEUZE, 2006).

will possible, intervening at the root of the cessation of desires.

For Freud, through the self-knowledge provided by clinical experience, it is possible to split the series of repetitions, rescuing content from the unconscious into the conscious, and thus reducing psychic determinism, increasing the capacity for choice, or just reducing repetition. It can be emphasized that the principle of the inverse link between repetition and consciousness [...] "the more the past is repeated, the less it is remembered, the less consciousness one has of remembering it - remember, elaborate the memory so as not to repeat it (DELEUZE, 2006). Thus, attempts to split with repetitions have always started from unconscious modifications, which would affect the faculty of judgement: A judgement would consist of us recognizing a proposition as true or false, an act of desire consists of us desiring it as good or avoiding it as bad (ZENTNER, 1995).

Even with all these alternatives available, for both Freud and Schopenhauer there will always be a primary Self determining a secondary Self.

8 FINAL CONSIDERATIONS

With this work we have had the opportunity to exercise the application of Deleuze's concepts in order to understand the approximations, distances and interlaps between the formulations created by Schopenhauer and Freud. The inseparability of the internal zones of communication dealt with throughout the research concerns the corresponding quadrangle of the theory of forgetting - will and repression - unconscious. But all this configuration and combination between one concept and another, in particular, can be redefined and reordered by other combinations. We have thus concluded that metaphysics and psychoanalysis are distinct systems, but their concepts can be co-created by the continuity between their ideas, even if they aim to solve other problems and occupy other territories. In a possible continuation of this work, it may be possible to further *emphasize* the fact that knowledge is often made through the interlocking of concepts and problems from different theories, especially with regard to the encounters and disagreements between Schopenhauer's metaphysics and Freud's metapsychology.

Bibliography

BIRMAN, J. **Freud & philosophy**. Rio de Janeiro: Jorge Zahar, 2003

CACCIOLA, M. L. M. and **Schopenhauer and the unconscious**. In:
KNOBLOCH, F. (org.) O inconsciente: varias leituras. Sao Paulo: Escuta, 1991.

CAROPRESO, F. Compulsion to repetition: from the "Project of a psychology" to "Beyond the pleasure principle", **Revista Natureza Humana**, v. 8, n. 2, 2006.

DELEUZE, G. GUATTARI, F. ***What is philosophy?*** Translated by Bento Prado Junior and Alberto Alonso Munoz. Rio de Janeiro: Editora 34, 1992.

DELEUZE, G. **Difference and repetition**. Rio de Janeiro: Graal; 2006.

FENICHEL, O. **Teoria Psicanalitica das Neuroses**. Translated by Samuel Penna Reis. Samuel Penna Reis. Rio de Janeiro: Imago, 1976.

FREUD, S. **Complete Psychological Works of Sigmund Freud.**
Directed by Jayme Salomao. Rio de Janeiro: Imago, 1996. Vol. XIV.

FREUD, S. **Complete Psychological Works of Sigmund Freud**.
Directed by Jayme Salomao. Rio de Janeiro: Imago, 1996. Vol. XI.

FREUD, S. **Complete Psychological Works of Sigmund Freud** . Directed by Jayme Salomao. Rio de Janeiro: Imago, 1996. Vol. XIX.

FULGENCIO, L. **Freud's metapsychological speculations**.

Human Nature, v. 5, n. 1, p. 129-173, 2003.

IANNACO, D. **Schopenhauer e i pazienti della Charite di Berlino** (1812-1813).IL Sogno della farfalla, Rivista di Psichiatria e Psicoterapia, Nuove Edizioni Romane: Roma, vol.4, 1998.

LAPLANCHE, J., & PONTALIS, J. B. ***The language of psychoanalysis.*** **Karnac Books**, 1998

LOPARIC, Z. **Beyond the unconscious: on the Heideggerian deconstruction of psychoanalysis**. Revista Natureza Humana, vol. 3, n.1, 2001.

OLIVEIRA, A. M. The psychology of Plato: on the theory of the human psyche (soul) in the dialogue Phaedrus, from the categories of the Apollonian and the Dionysian. **Plethos**, Rio de Janeiro, n. 1, v. 2, p. 176-194, 2012.

PLATO, A. **Republic**. Translated by Enrico Corvisieri. Sao Paulo: Nova Cultural, 1997.

RAIKOVIC, P. **Freud's dogmatic sleep: Kant, Schopenhauer, Freud**. Rio de Janeiro: Zahar, 1996.

ROTHE-NEVES, R.; NEVES, A. Freud and forgetfulness in Marcel Zentner's Die Flucht ins Vergegessen. **Psicologia: Reflexao e Critica**. vol.15, n°.2, 2002.

SCHOPENHAUER, Arthur. **The World as Will and Representation**. 2nd ed. M. S. Sa Correia. Rio de Janeiro: Contraponto, 2004.

ZENTNER, Marcel. **Die flucht ins vergessen: die anfange der psychoanalyse freuds bei schopenhauer**. Darmstald: Wiss]

Enschaftliche Buchgesellschaft, 1995.

Printed by Books on Demand GmbH, Norderstedt / Germany